WHEN CONDITIONS WERE MET, THE SEED BECAME A FOREST

First published in 2015 by

Copyright ©2015 Tshepo Nketle, The Duke Publishers

ISBN: 978-0-620-65919-2

Tshepo Nketle has asserted his rights to be identified as the author of this work in accordance with the Copyright, Designs and Pattern Act 1998

All rights reserved.
This book was printed in the Republic of South Africa. No part of this publication may be reproduced, stored in a retrieval system or transmitted in any form or by any means, electronic, mechanical, photocopying, recording or otherwise without the written permission of the copyright owner.

Cover designed by: The Duke Inventions

The Duke of Happiness

Table of Contents

Content	Page
Acknowledgements	7
About the Author	9
Dedications	11
A Crazy Old Man	17
A Mistakeful Head Master	23
A troubled woman	29
A naughty old man	35
Old Clothes	41
Why The Duke of Happiness?	45
How bad do you want to pee?	55
What will you harvest?	61
The Dog and the Rooster	65
Soup kitchen	69
Lotto ticket	73
A smart student	77
We are all connected	81
The seed became a forest	87
The delivery boy	91

The Seed became a Forest

The Duke of Happiness

Acknowledgements

I'd love to acknowledge the assistance from The Duke Publishers team, you guys are the best. Lucia Anderson, Lady Hope and Belinda Swartz, it wouldn't have been the same without you guys, thank you team Duke. I know it wasn't easy to be part of the "just founded" publishing house at first. Yet you guys stayed with me through it all. With all your hard work, The Duke Publishers has now published so many books and so many Authors. Thank you!

I deeply acknowledge the support that I get from my wife, Bulelwa Nketle. Sometimes I travel for a good couple of days and leave her all by herself, yet she understands every step of the journey that I have chosen and she stands by my side unconditionally. Love you cutey!

Allow me acknowledge the support that I get from my facebook friends. I cannot describe the importance of the role that they had played in the growth of both The Duke and Tshepo Nketle. They believe in me. They stand for me. They

The Seed became a Forest

support me as if I am one of their own. Thank you guys and girls, your kindness won't go unnoticed.

I acknowledge the support that I get from my family. I know sometimes I can be very difficult, but through it all, my family is always behind me.

About the Author

Tshepo Nketle, better known as The Duke of Happiness was born and raised in Cape Town, Khayelitsha. Elder Son to Mr. Thabo Ernest Nketle and Matshepo Florence Nketle and rooting from a small village called Fletcherville in Mount Fletcher, in the Eastern Province of South Africa.

Primary schooled at Ummangaliso Public Primary School, secondary schooled at Matthew Goniwe Memorial High School. Tshepo Nketle is a proud Chrysalis Academy 2004 Delta graduate.

The Duke is an Author of many books to even mention. Including the game changer, Earn Your Freedom, The TINSTAHL – Trilogy, The Greatness of a Single Mom, Lessons From the Past and many others.

The Duke is an Inspirational Speaker and a Spiritual Messenger. The Duke founded one of the fastest growing publishing houses in Cape Town, The Duke Publishers. The

The Seed became a Forest

Duke is a Managing Director at The Duke Clothing and the umbrella body of it all, The Duke Empire.

The Duke of Happiness

Dedications

I dedicate this book to my late father, Thabo Ernest Nketle and his loving wife Matshepo Florence Nketle. Daddy, wherever you are, I know you are smiling down as you see your son creating a legacy that will inspire millions of people. In my heart you will forever live.

The Seed became a Forest

The Duke of Happiness

Introduction

It takes a village to raise a child and when that child is raised well, it will take him to feed the entire village.

The most valuable and important things in life have very humble beginnings. Yet as you follow their background story you begin to realise that it were those humble beginnings that actually shaped and added value onto things. It is those hardships and sacrifices that made it worthy. The TINSTAHL tells us that, in the midst of darkness is where light is born, light is not born of light. A torch in the sun is worthless, yet that very same torch is worth every piece of ounce in the dark room.

I was inspired to write these stories and share them with you. The aim is to make you understand and realise that the circumstances of yesterday and the challenges of today are what is shaping the brightness of your future. I

The Seed became a Forest

hope you will find inspiration in these stories in the same way that I have. If you read them with an open heart, these stories will touch your soul and inspire your life in such an amazing way. As it stands, no one had ever read this entire book without crying (or at least get emotional). Not in a negative way but in an inspiring way.

It has always been in the culture of The Duke to begin my every book with The Duke's Prayer. To those who wonder, I am very spiritual person and I believe a prayer can change any negative energy and turn it to pure light. In this regard therefore, I transmute any and every negative feeling and energy and turning it into pure light, in the name of love.

The Duke's Prayer:
> "Blessed Father, **I'm sorry** for doubting You, Your ways and laws and for doubting myself every now and then. **Please forgive me** for letting Your property suffer the illusions and the opinions of the outside appearance and for every suffering and misery that I have consciously and unconsciously caused for any

The Duke of Happiness

of your creatures, from the beginning of my creation to the present at any place, time, event and anyone else who may be involved directly or indirectly. **I love You** Father. And **thank You** for all you have done for me including those that I'm still waiting to receive, bad, to strengthen and guide me so I could learnt to let go, and good, to become the best of myself so I could make the most of other people. Namaste."

The Seed became a Forest

The Duke of Happiness

A Crazy Old Man

The Seed became a Forest

At the summer of a very odd year, an old man dicided to do a very strange thing. He woke up in the morning and too a walk to the dam, but he didn't use the normal path, he created his own path straight from his house to the dam. And when he got to the dam, he sat down for five minutes and had a smoke. Straight after, he walked back home. Then he went to invest some time into his garden. He did this insane thing every day, three times a day and everytime he came back, he worked on his garden.

Summer came to an end and it was Automn, the onld man didn't show any signs of ever stopping this madness. Now people we beginning to notice and as nosey as people are, they send their kids to follow the old man and see exactly what he does at the dam three times a day. The kids came back to their parents and told them that the old man had clearly lost it because all he does at the dam is having a smoke and then head back home.

The Duke of Happiness

Winter approached, people were beginning to talk. Some gossiped against the old man, telling others that the old man was crazy and needed to be taken to some mental institution. Some judged the old man, others suggested that the old man should leave the village because they no longer feel safe with an insane old man in their village.

At the end of Winter came Spring and still there were no improvements, the old man had made the situation even worse. He had now added another trip a day to the dam, meaning that he was now going four times a day top the dam. There was still no one with any slight idea of the reason why the old man keeps walking to the dam, except for the perceptions and judgements that the old man was insane. People were now all united against the old man, they had all agreed to chase the old man out of their village for their children's safety. It's funny how people can all agree to such insensitive decisions, but who the hell am I? Anyways, they sent people at night to frighten the old mna so he could pack and go. But the old man didn't go, he woke up in the morning and continued with his routine.

The Seed became a Forest

Then it was Summer again. Heavy rains started to pour. They poured so heavily that the dam was over-filled. Then the water from the dam began to flow onto the old man's trail. Water followed the trail all the way to the old man's garden (where he always began and ended his daily journey to the river) into the whole that the old man had been digging in his garden all along. In two days, the old man's small dam was full. Then in no time, the rain season approached an end. The entire village depended on the water that's in the dam for all their needs. Within weeks, the dam ran dry and the village was in a huge crisis of water shortage. People couldn't help noticing that the old man was no longer taking his daily walks to the dam. They also noticed that, even though the Village was out of water, the old man was constantly watering his garden.

The Village elders went to see the old man to find out where he gets water from. The old man told them that for four seasons, he took a walk three to four times a day to the dam, with intentions of making a trail for water to be able to flow to his garden, then in his garden he made a big whole to store all the water that flowed from the dam. The elders of the Village asked the

The Duke of Happiness

old man if he could be so kind to share some of his water with the Village, and the old man said he didn't do it for himself, he did it for the entire village, he realised that there were too many judgements and condemtions in the Village, the Village needed someone who will love it as it is, without judging or grudging it.

The Village School was named after the old man.

The Seed became a Forest

The Duke of Happiness

A Mistakeful Head Master

The Seed became a Forest

A not so very long time ago in one of the highest boarding schools in the southern hemisphere, a Head Master (Principal) wanted to discuss the performance and behaviour of one of his students with the student's parents. So, he wrote a letter to give to the student so that the student could give it to his parents upon visitation. But he forgot to bring the letter with to the dining hall during supper. After dining, he asked the student for his room number so he (The Head Master) could deliver the letter. The student told The Head Master that his room was number two on third floor (Room 2, 3rd Floor). The Head Master went to his office to fetch the letter and as he entered the lift, he wasn't sure whether the student said room two, third floor or room three, second floor. It only made sense to him if he first goes to room three, second floor (Room 3, 2nd Floor), for if that is the correct room, he will save a trip to the higher floor.

The Head Master knocked at room three, second floor (Room3, 2nd Floor) but no one answered the door. He

The Duke of Happiness

knocked a few times knowing that all the students must be in their rooms at that time of the night but there was still no answer. The Head Master opened the door, fortunately it wasn't locked. He was so shocked to see a student standing on a chair with a hanging rope from the ceiling around his neck. The Student was just ready to kick the chair and his life would have been history. The Head Master immediately approached the student and slowly removed the rope from his neck and with a big sigh, sat him down. Then he asked "What is wrong my son, why would you want to take your own life?". The student replied with tears "I made a mistake, a mistake that disappointed a lot of people, my parents, my girlfriend and myself. I don't deserve to live, I deserve to die. I'm a disgrace to my friends and family. I keep making mistakes over and over again".

Then The Head Master said "That's the beauty of life! MIstakes are what life is all about. Every Master who had ever walked on this planet will gladly tell you that there are no such things as mistakes, all that happens, happens because it has to happen. Nothing can ever happen if it is not supposed to happen. The Sun knows that it has to rise from the East and set to the West. In

The Seed became a Forest

the millions of years of existence, never had the sun decided to rise from the West and set to the East. That didn't happen because it is not meant to happen. But when the storm hits and destroys buildings and structures, that's not a mistake, that is what has to happen. We may not know the reason why it happens, but the Universe does. Every time you make a mistake, you learn a lesson. Every mistake is an opportunity for you to become a better and greater person. Every time you screw up, that's your life's greatest teacher saying to you "Good morning class!".

I am older now, but if I could be given an opportunity to be at your age again, I'd screw up more and I won't waste a second regretting it. It is only through mistakes that we grow, learn and become great. Life is not a lesson, but mistakes always bring us lessons to learn in life, and opportunities to become great. Look at me, I feel great now for saving a young man's life but I am here by mistake. I was meant to be in room two, third floor. But if it wasn't for that mistake, you would have been a dead boy by now. So, you thought a mistake was a bad thing, yet a mistake just spared your life. In this

The Duke of Happiness

regard therefore, this is a mistake saying to you "take another look at me".

The Seed became a Forest

The Duke of Happiness

A troubled woman

The Seed became a Forest

A troubled woman went to see The Duke for consultation. She wanted The Duke's advice and as always, The Duke was willingly available to assist and advise her. The woman seemed confident but deep down, The Duke could see that, she was hurting and confused. She greeted The Duke and The Duke asked her to take a sit. She then told The Duke that the reason why she came to see him is because things are not going well in her life. In what way? Asked The Duke. Somehow I don't get the things that I want in life, the woman said, I always seem to get the things that I do not want and I keep wondering why.

What do you want? Asked The Duke. I don't want a man who snores, said the woman, yet I keep attracting one. I don't want a man who sits at home the whole day watching TV. I don't want a man who drinks. I don't want to keep staying at my parents' house. I don't want to be broke. I don't want hard labour work. I don't want to keep asking my parents for money. I don't want to be dependant. I don't want… I don't want… I don't want…

The Duke of Happiness

Yet all the things that I had just outlined to you are the very things that keep on happening in my life.

You are such a wonderful creator, said The Duke. What do you mean? Asked the woman. Look at all the things that you had created and still keep creating, answered The Duke. If you can create all the things that you had just told me, asked The Duke, don't you think that's good enough an evidence that you can create their opposite too? I'm not sure if I still follow you Duke, proclaimed the woman. It's simple, said The Duke, the reason why you keep experiencing the things that you do not want is because you spend most of your time thinking and talking about the things that you do not want. That alone is a powerful creative process. The Universe doesn't know what you want, it gives to you, solely, the things that you spend more time thinking and talking about, whether you want them or not. With this regard therefore, concluded The Duke, you keep attracting the things you don't want because The Universe thinks you are passionate about them. Now let's reverse the process. What do you want? Asked The Duke. If it's a house you want say you want a house, said The Duke.

The Seed became a Forest

Well, I want a shack Duke because I can't afford a house, said the woman. No, no, no young lady, said The Duke, you don't limit The Universe. It has been around long before you and it will surely be around way after you. Whether you can or can't afford it was not the question, said The Duke, the question was what do you want? When you put it clear to The Universe what you want, you let The Universe show you ways and means to attain it. If there are no ways and means, The Universe will create them. So, how you will attain it is not your part to worry about, that's The Universe's job. All that you have to do is to say what you want allow The Universe to bring it to you.

You didn't have means to attract a snoring man, yet because you kept thinking and talking about him, The Universe brought him to you. When you were a child, you never had means to buy food, yet The Universe kept you fed until today. In the same way, keep talking and thinking about the house that you want. How does it look on the outside? How does it look in the inside? Where is it situated? How many rooms is it? What colour is the paint? All those details are what you must

The Duke of Happiness

keep thinking and talking about and The Universe will make means. Same applies to the man you want. What kind of a man do you want? How tall is he? How does his voice sound? How does he look? How does he sound when sleeping? And most importantly, what are you willing to offer him? All those details... Keep thinking ant talking about them and slowly but surely, the universe will attract to you the man who is your dream man. Do you want a job? What kind of a job? What are you passionate about? How can you turn that into servicing other people and then they can remunerate you in return to your services?

Those are the details to spend more time thinking and talking about, said The Duke.

Imagine you were sitting with God, said The Duke, and God told you to ask for anything that you had ever wanted in life, except for money, what would it be? Write it down, proclaimed The Duke. And do not limit your imagination, concluded The Duke, if an aeroplane is one of them, why not?

The Seed became a Forest

The woman left a better woman with better and bigger dreams. She was ready to live the life that she deserved. For so long, she was trapped in the box, without even knowing it. So, don't worry about how you will get what you desire. Just desire and The Universe will create the way.

The Duke of Happiness

A naughty old man

The Seed became a Forest

A very old man was troubling his village so much. He was the oldest in the village and for that reason he demanded that everyone should respect him. He respected no one in the village, claiming that he is the one who should be respected as he was the oldest man in the village. He greeted no one, he wanted people to greet him first before he can greet them back, claiming that he was the oldest in the village and, therefore, people should treat him as such. The way he spoke to people was harsh, commanding and disrespectful. He always expected people to agree with all his views and opinions because he was the oldest in the village.

Whenever he wanted something, he expected everyone to run around and do it for him. He would sometimes do annoying things like waking up in the morning, go to his garden and sing out loud while other villagers are still sleeping. Because he believed that as the oldest man in the village he had every right to do whatever he wanted, because he believed that he was the one who should be respected not the other way round.

The Duke of Happiness

Slowly but surely, the villagers began to lose respect on the old man. All of a sudden, no one greeted him anymore. He noticed also that whenever he "orders" children to do things (like fetching water from the river) for him, they became cheeky and completely took him for granted. Whenever there was village rituals and traditional ceremonies, the old man was no longer given that special treatment as he was the oldest in the village, he was completely taken for granted. Other village elders refused to dine with him, they sent him to dine with the youngsters. But the youngsters refused to accept him too. He would end up dining all by himself. The old man was now a laughing stock whom everyone saw like an idiot.

At that moment, the old man realised that something was wrong. He decided to go see the wise Master of the village. He told the Master that the villagers no longer respect him and for that reason they should be punished. He claimed that no one is greeting him anymore and even children refuse to fetch him water from the river and as the elder of the village, he demanded justice.

The Seed became a Forest

How cruel of these villagers, said the wise Master. Don't they know that it is compulsory that they respect their elders? I will have to apologise on their behalf elder, said the wise Master, they have lost our ways and for that reason they will all be punished. The old man's face started to glow with excitement, seeing that the wise Master is on his side. However, proclaimed the wise Master, in order for my plan to work, I will need you to be humble for a while and demonstrate to them what it's like to respect a person. When they had seen that from you (as their elder), I will therefore impose severe punishment to every villager, except for you of course.

This was a very easy task to an old man. He accepted it with all his heart. All he needed was to just pretend as if he was respecting everyone in the village. He just needed to greet everyone first. He just needed to pretend to be smiling whenever he greets or talk to any villager. He just needed to use the words "please", "I'm sorry" and "thank you" for a while, until the Master punishes the entire village. And then after, he thought, he would go back to his initial habit. The Master asked the old man to do this for as long as he wants. The

The Duke of Happiness

longer he does it, the harder the punishment will be towards the rest of the villagers. Because the old man wanted the villagers to pay deeply, he was committed to doing this for a very long time.

The first week went by. The villagers were so amazed at how the old man had become. All of a sudden, the villagers thought, the old man had manners. Weeks went by. Weeks became months. The longer the old man respected others, he noticed, the more at peace he felt. The beautiful thing about a smile is that you cannot fake it for a very long time. One thing about caring is that you cannot be able to pretend, it's either you are caring or you are not. The more you act as a caring person, the more of a caring person you become. The old man even offered to help where help was needed, something that he had never done in his entire life. And from all these acts, the villagers slowly began to respect the old man in a way that no person had ever respected him before. Children now offered to fetch water for him, others even offered to wash his clothes. Everyone in the village wanted to please the old man in their own unique way. All of a sudden, the village elders valued the old man's opinions and views. The old man felt a deep feeling of love, respect, value, peace and appreciation – something that he had never experienced nor felt before.

The village Master paid a visit to the old man and told him that it was now time for the villagers to be punished. What have they done? Asked the old man.

Respect is earned, not forced. People reflect back to you what you send out to them. If you want to be loved, start loving. If you want to be respected, start respecting. If you want to be valued, start valuing. If you want to be appreciated, start appreciating. If you want people to comment on your facebook status, start commenting on theirs. The Universe gives to you what you had accepted as being true in your life. You may never be honoured if you do not honour. You may never be helped if you never help.

The Duke of Happiness

Old Clothes!

The Seed became a Forest

A young boy, at an age of 5 to 6 years, used to go to Retreat with his mother every Saturday. His mother would throw him on her back and they would walk down the streets of Retreat shouting "OLD CLOTHES!". All they were asking for was old clothes. They were not asking for food nor for money, just old clothes. It didn't matter how cold it was. It didn't matter how burning the son was. It didn't matter how windy or rainy it was, the young boy's mother would throw him on her back and they would walk up the streets of Retreat, knocking from one door to another, asking for old clothes.

After they had collected the clothes, they would take them home, his mother would wash them and they would share among them (the boy, his mother and his father). Whatever that was left over would be sold for a few extra cash to buy food and toiletries.

The boy learnt something from the experience of knocking door to door, asking for old clothes. Sometimes they would knock at some doors and be

The Duke of Happiness

rejected like evil. Some other times people would send dogs to chase the boy and his mother away. Some people would shout and curse at them before they even knock. Some others would just ignore them as if nobody was knocking. But there are those people who would open their doors for the young boy and his mother. They would welcome them with warm hearts and even offer them something to drink. Some would give them the old clothes while others, who didn't have old clothes, would offer anything that they had. From that experience, the young boy learnt that one may never know what to expect behind a closed door until they knock. He learnt that one door may have rejection behind it. Other door may have cruelty behind it. Maybe the next door might have anger behind it. But that doesn't mean there are no more doors with love, peace and laughter behind them, one just needed to keep knocking until they knock at the right door at the right time.

In whatever you do, never give up. As long as you wake up still breathing, keep knocking. You may have knocked all your life without success, then keep knocking some more. You will never know what's behind any door until you knock.

The Seed became a Forest

I know the boy turned out to be a big and wise man, because it is that young boy who wrote this book. He is now known as The Duke of Happiness.

Why The Duke of Happiness?

The Seed became a Forest

Before his death, my father had a very strong desire to be rich. He had no way of doing it in mind and by chance, happened to see an advert on the local newspaper, about some Nigerian doctor who was capable of making people rich. My father phoned the doctor and asked him what the catch was and the doctor said there was no catch, my father should just pay a preparation fee and then receive his money, and the doctor would then take his share after my father had received the money. My father asked if where the money came from and the doctor said it came from the ancestors. Then my father paid five hundred rands into the doctor's bank for preparation and the doctor sent some sticks over to my father and told him what to do with the sticks. Oh yes, my father was a very deep believer in ancestors.

We then followed the instructions and did everything the Nigerian doctor told us to do. The following day, was supposed to be the best day ever for our family. We were to be millionaires. I even went window shopping

The Duke of Happiness

for a car that I would come back the following day to buy. We were ready to sell our old house and buy ourselves a very big and beautiful house. Would you blame us? We were to become millionaires the following day. The night of that day was the longest of my life. I didn't sleep well that night; I was nervous and excited at the same time. I could hear my father coughing in his room in the middle of the night. He definitely wasn't sleeping as well. At 6am I heard his voice shouting "Tsheeeepo!", "Ntateee!" I replied (*Ntate in Sesotho means Dad*). Then he said nothing. That's how he always called me. He would just shout my name and wait for my response and then say nothing. He had never shouted "come here!" or "where are you?" no, not my dad. And I always knew that, I had to go to him whenever he shouts my name. He asked me to open the box where we had put the magic sticks and check if the ancestors' money is not in yet. I did and there was nothing, only sticks were there; thin, long and black sticks were all that was left in the box of our family's hope.

My father phoned the Nigerian doctor to find out what the matter was and the doctor was to check with the

The Seed became a Forest

ancestors and get back to us. Later that day, the doctor phoned and told us that our ancestors demand two white chickens and a bottle of brandy from us and then we should get the money. The money we were promised was seven million rands. So my father had to deposit an extra two hundred rands for the two white chickens and a bottle of brandy. The following morning, my father shouted my name and I ran quickly to his room. He asked me to open the box where we had put the magic sticks and check if the ancestors' money is not in yet. I did and there was still nothing, only sticks were there, thin, long and black sticks were all that was left in the box of our family's hope.

My father was very angry. He called the Nigerian doctor and asked him what the problem could be. Again, the Nigerian doctor told us he was to check with the ancestors and then come back to us. We waited the entire day and the entire night. Ancestors must be really far hey. We phoned the Nigerian doctor but to our surprise, his phone was off. I started to lose hope but my father was still certain that the doctor would phone back, and he did. He phoned back the following night and told us that he was with the ancestors the whole

The Duke of Happiness

time and they were telling him that we deserve to receive more than seven million rands. He told us that our ancestors had offered sixty million rands and they only require us to sacrifice a white cow for them. How much was a white cow then? It was only eight thousand rands. Who wouldn't sacrifice eight thousand rands for sixty million rands? My dad was broke but he made three different loans from three different loan sharks. He was desperate; we were desperate for change. He deposited the money into the Nigerian doctor's bank. The Nigerian doctor promised us that we were to be sixty million rands richer, the following morning. We started hoping again. The following morning, my father shouted my name and I woke up and ran straight to his room. He asked me to open the box where we had put the magic sticks and check if the ancestors' money is not in yet. I did and there was still nothing, only sticks were there; thin, long and black sticks were all that was left in the box of our family's hope.

I phoned the Nigerian doctor this time. My father was too upset to speak to him. When I asked him what the matter was, he said the very same thing, he was to check with the ancestors and come back to us. Hours went by, a day and a night went by. Days went by and the Nigerian doctor was not phoning us. When we phone him, his phone was off. We were so upset and depressed at the same time. After a couple of days, we finally got hold of him. He told us he was busy with the ancestors. I asked him where the money was and he said the ancestors had released the money but it had to be cleansed. They required a white goat to cleanse the money. The white goat was eight hundred rands. My father made another loan from a loan shark, hoping to pay them back with interest. Oh yes, we really persisted. We deposited the money into this doctor's account and waited again for the following morning. The morning came and my father shouted my name. I ran to his room as usual. He then asked me to open the box where we had put the magic sticks and check if the ancestors' money is not in yet. I did and there was still nothing, only sticks were there; thin, long and black sticks were all that was left in the box of our family's hope.

Again, we phoned the Nigerian doctor. This time, his phone was ringing but he just was not picking up our calls. When I restricted my number, he picked it up and when he noticed it was my voice, he hung up on me.

The Duke of Happiness

Not once and not twice but many times. Days went by and weeks went by. I had lost all the hopes of ever becoming a millionaire already. Out of nowhere, he phoned us. He told us that our money was ready but we needed to bribe the bank manager for he would phone the police if people were to deposit sixty million rands cash in the bank. I asked if what the bank has to do with anything and he said sixty million rands was too much for his magic rats to transport it to our house so the bank was the only way of transfer. When we asked how much the bank manager needed, he said fifty thousand rands.

I know what you are thinking. Why didn't he take fifty thousand rands from the sixty million rands? And yes, I asked him that but he said the money could not be used before it was at the bank and those were the ancestors' rules.

My father and I knew at that moment that we were being played. It was clear that the whole story was made up. There was no ancestors' money and there was no sixty million rands. My father started to stress. How was he going to pay back all the money that he had

The Seed became a Forest

borrowed from loan sharks? In less than a week, my father's feet started to swell and the doctor told him they were caused by stressing too much. On Monday morning, the 14th of January 2008, my father died of heart failure. When I heard the news, I started hearing Mike and the Mechanics lyrics *"I wasn't there that morning, when my father passed away, I didn't get to tell him all the things I had to say"*...

That day, was the saddest day of my life, and it was my life's turning point.

Poverty can put you into places that you had never thought you could ever be. It can make you do things that you had never imagined yourself doing. I always had a desire to share this experience with the rest of the world, but I didn't know how and I didn't know where. I am sharing this story with you today, not because I want to keep you stuck in my memories but because I want you to know that, things could always be worse. I know there are still a lot of people in South Africa who are still falling into this trap of paying some doctors to make them rich. The question is, if they can make people rich, why can't they make themselves rich? Of course, that

The Duke of Happiness

had never crossed my mind when I was also within their boundaries.

After my father had passed away, I was the hope of the family. I was all that was left. Then I figured; we trusted in sticks to bring happiness and abundance into our family. So, according to our thinking and expectations, sticks were supposed to bring us happiness. But the sticks and my father are no more. My family now trusts in me to bring peace, happiness, wealth, prosperity and abundance into the family. I then decided I might as well call myself *"Sticks" (the bringer of happiness)* for I was the hope of the family after my father had left and sticks were no more. So, "STIX – The Duke of Happiness" is all that is left; thin, long and black STIX is all that is left in the box of our family's hope.

One last thing; my name "Tshepo" in Sesotho means "Hope"... This all just comes together, doesn't it?

The Seed became a Forest

The Duke of Happiness

How bad do you want to pee?

The Seed became a Forest

A few years after his graduation, a high school student went to see his Teacher. The Teacher was so happy to see his student but he could see that something was bothering him. They sat done to have a chat. Before they began, the Teacher ordered the student to fill a litre jar with water and bring it, and then lock the door so no one can interrupt. The student followed orders and brought a jar of cold water and the door key to his high school teacher.

Now as they started talking about what was bothering the student, the Teacher kept encouraging the student to drink a glass of water. The student was telling the Teacher that his life is a mess and things are never working out for him. I tried everything, said the student, but nothing seems to work for me. As the Teacher was carefully listening, he kept nodding his head and encouraged the student to have another glass of water. The student would have a glass of water and then carry on with his unfortunate life story.

The Duke of Happiness

In an hour's time, the student had emptied the jar and he started feeling a desire to go to the gentlemen's room. He asked the Teacher to excuse him. Certainly, said the Teacher. The student quickly walked towards the door so he could make his way to the toilets. But the door was locked. He forgot that he locked the door and handed the key over to the Teacher. He looked at the teacher and asked for the key. I don't have the key, said the Teacher, you locked the door. But I gave the key to you, said the student. No, you didn't, said the Teacher. Then the student began to doubt if he really gave the key to the Teacher. So, they both decided to look for the key. Time was going and the student's desire to go to the toilets kept getting stronger and stronger. Now the skin colour of the student had begun to be paler and paler. After thirty minutes of trying to find the key, the Teacher realised that the student had reached the peak of the moment. Then he took the key out of his pocket and said, hey you were right, you did give me the key, here, go. The student took the key and quickly ran to the toilets to release the water out of his body.

When he came back, the Teacher asked how it felt like to be desperate. It feels horrible, said the student, you

The Seed became a Forest

get to a stage where you are prepared to do anything, a stage where you don't care how the next person looks at you. I almost peed at the corner of your classroom, concluded the student, everything else went to the background, what mattered the most in my entire life at that moment was that I wanted to pee. That's how life is supposed to be, explained the Teacher, when you want something you must want it so bad that you are prepared to risk anything to get it. You got to be hungry. Don't just wish for success and happiness. Don't just hope your life will eventually become a perfect life. Be hungry for the kind of life that you want. You got to sleep your desire. Eat your desire. Drink your desire. Talk your desire. Walk your desire.

You got to be hungry.

In the same way you were so desperate to go pee, you got to be hungry for your success and happiness to manifest. Make no room for excuses. You didn't have excuses to go pee. You didn't care how you did it. All that mattered was that you had to do it.

The Duke of Happiness

You got to be hungry for success. You got to be hungry for happiness. And life will bend to your command.

The Seed became a Forest

The Duke of Happiness

What will you harvest?

The Seed became a Forest

Two men were each given ten maize meals. They were allowed to use them in whatever way that pleased them.

The first man used them to make a meal for his family for two nights. For two consecutive nights, his family was filled with joy and satisfaction because they went to bed with a filling meal. But then on the third day they went back to the first square.

The second man planted the rest of his maize meals into the ground. His family was starving, children went to bed with empty stomachs, yet this man went ahead and buried all his maize meals under the ground. People of the village were talking and asking questions. How can a man in his rightful mind plant all his maize meal while his family is starving? His wife didn't agree with his plan in the first place, but he went ahead and followed it anyway. Among the reasons why he shouldn't put maize under the ground, suggested his wife, was that birds might just dig all of it out and eat it. She also feared that

The Duke of Happiness

children might dig them out and play with them. But the man continued with his plan anyway.

The man had now lost people's respect. Even his wife and family was no longer respecting him because they saw him as a fool who buried all his maize meal while his children die in hunger. In five to six months time, the man harvested hundreds of thousands more maize meals than the ten he had had planted. On the day of harvest, he suddenly became everyone's favourite. His wife was suddenly the proudest wife in the village. His children couldn't wish for a better father. And all the women of the village wished they had a husband like him. The man fed his family and later his village for as long he lived. He never ate all the maize. He always left some of it to be planted so that they can harvest again in the following year.

You reap what you sow. Never sacrifice the future for the temporary satisfaction of the present. Rather suffer the short term pains in return of the long term pleasures. Work like a slave so when you harvest, you can live like a King

The Seed became a Forest

The Duke of Happiness

The dog and the rooster!

The Seed became a Forest

Once a dog and a rooster were chatting, in fact, the rooster was bragging to the dog, telling it that it is more important to their master than the dog. The rooster counted its reasons to think and believe that it had more meaning to the master that the dog. I wake the master every morning, said the rooster. I make more chicks for the master to keep feeding his family. Even when I'm dead, unlike you, the master won't throw me into the bush, he will use me to feed his family. So, I am important to the master when I'm alive and I am also important when I'm dead. And you on the other side, exclaimed the rooster, are just wasting the master's food. You are just good for barking, eating my cousins' bones, finishing the master's food, and dying. Even when you are dead, to show you how useless you are, the master throws you into the middle of the bush, concluded the rooster.

The dog was stunned. It couldn't believe it was that useless. Yet deep down, everything that the rooster said made sense. This troubled the dog, and the rooster kept saying it over and over again. The dog believed the

The Duke of Happiness

rooster and the dog began falling apart. It decided to take all its belongings and leave at once. Just as it was sneaking out, the master caught it and asked where the dog was heading. I'm heading north, said the dog, the rooster is right, I serve no purpose in this home. The rooster wakes you up in the morning, it produces more chicks for you to feed your family and it still gives supper even if it's dead. I only bark, eat and die. And I get thrown away when I'm dead. I'm useless. The rooster is way better than I am.

Perhaps you are right, said the master. But if you leave, my children will never be safe again. By the way, there are thieves in this village, they steal mostly roosters. Have you ever wondered why they never tried to steal my rooster? It's because they fear you. Even the rooster knows that, it just wants to feel superior. You are my best friend and the protector of this home. Without you, we are doomed.

Never allow anyone make you believe that you don't have a purpose or their purpose is better than yours. Everyone has a purpose and each person's purpose is different and unique, yet perfect. Go ahead and serve

The Seed became a Forest

your purpose, that's what you were placed here for. Nothing less, nothing more.

The Duke of Happiness

Soup kitchen!

The Seed became a Forest

Once there was a down town soup kitchen where poor people would go for their supper. They would gather outside while each person waits to be called in. Upon entering, they would each receive a plate of warm food and a cup of warm soup.

This one time, as the pointer was pointing at the people one at a time to come inside, he pointed at this random guy, as the guy was ready to go in, the kitchen Master shouted "No! Not that one". This was very strange because the kitchen Master had a reputation of a very kind old man. Everyone was stunned. They random guy, with disappointment all over his eyes, went back outside.

The pointer continued pointing and instructing the pointed people to come in for their dinner. He pointed and pointed and pointed until there was no one left to point but the random guy. The pointer instructed him to come in again but the kitchen Master yelled "No! I said not that one!!!"

The Duke of Happiness

The random guy was confused and disappointed at the same time. Hunger was also getting the best of him. He immediately decided that he will go in and apologise to the kitchen Master for whatever he may have said or done that caused the kitchen Master to hate him. As he approached the kitchen Master, he looked at his eyes and said "*Master, you gave everyone their supper but me. What have I done to you? Why do you hate me so much?*"

The Master looked at the random guy with a smile and said "*There's one that I am specially preparing for you. I am still busy with it, hence you see me standing in the kitchen. Everyone here loves their chicken. I know how allergic you are to chicken hence I am then preparing a vegetarian dish for you. I do not hate you, I love you. That is why I am preparing your dish myself.*"

YOURS IS STILL COMING

Maybe you have been praying for years and you can't seem to succeed. Your success is still being prepared.

The Seed became a Forest

Maybe your friends or school mates are now driving expensive cars while you are still walking, yours is still coming.

Maybe you just never seem to get the job, no matter how many times you apply or submit your CV. Know this my brother and my sister, YOURS IS STILL COMING. The Master is busy preparing it for you.

The Duke of Happiness

Lotto ticket

The Seed became a Forest

My father once told me a story of a man who prayed every morning before leaving his bed and every evening before falling asleep. He prayed for one thing, one thing only, to win lotto. Saturday came and the lotto draw took place, unfortunately, the man didn't win. He continued praying. He prayed with energy and with commitment. He believed that God would make him win that lotto one day. But that day just seemed to delay. Another lotto draw day (Saturday) came and the man hadn't won. Did he give up? No he didn't! The man continued praying. He prayed even harder. He even started fasting. It was now a month later and he still hadn't won. The process went on and on. Harder and stronger each time.

A year went by, the man still hadn't won the lotto. He remembered that God sometimes takes his own time to answer people's prayers. So, he continued praying and fasting for lotto winnings. He even went to the mountains to pray for days. Yet God didn't seem to come to this man's rescue. Years went by and the man still persisted. He really believed deep down that God

The Duke of Happiness

would one day make him win lotto. But that one day just didn't come. After ten years of this process, the man unfortunately died of hunger.

When the man got to heaven he kneed before God and claimed "My God, for ten years - for TEN consecutive years I had prayed and fasted that you help me win lotto. But here I am, dead of hunger. Why didn't you come to my rescue?" Then God said "My poor son, I tried. For ten years I had aligned all the lotto numbers according to your thoughts and desires. If only you had bought a lotto ticket".

For the ten years that the man was praying and fasting, he never - not even once - bought a lotto ticket.

God only helps those who are willing to help themselves. To those who complain, God adds more things to complain about. In order for things to happen, you got to make things happen. Things don't just happen.

The Seed became a Forest

The Duke of Happiness

A smart student

The Seed became a Forest

A very intelligent and smart student was beginning to fall apart. He was the only one mastering every level of the martial arts and for some reason, his performance began to drop. Sometimes he would be late for practice and even when he is at the practice, one could tell that his mind and heart was elsewhere. This bothered his Master so much because The Master knew the potential that was within this student and he couldn't bear seeing all that potential going down with water. This affected many other students who were looking up to this student as well because the truth of the matter is that each person's energy affects everyone in the room. The Master tried to discipline him a couple of times but none of that made any difference. The harder the punishment, the cheekier the student became.

After careful observations and considerations, The Master decided it was high time he had a serious word with his student. This time, not with intentions of disciplining the student, but with intentions of reaching out to him. The Master summoned the student and they sat down for a serious talk. "Something is bothering you

The Duke of Happiness

my child. Please talk to me", said The Master. The student looked around to see if there wasn't anyone listening before he could open his heart to his Master and after a couple of seconds, the student opened up to The Master. "It's the other students, they say I think I'm better than the rest of them just because I master all the stages of the art. They say I'm no better, I'm just a trump that happened to be a fast learner. On top of that they added that this spirit of mine will only last for a while because people of my kind are never completely good at anything", said the student with sorrow written on his eyes.

This broke The Master's heart. Without allowing emotions control him, The Master comforted the student "You see my child, in life there will always be critics. Even though they think they are here to break us but the truth of the matter is that they are here to help us grow. Without critics we may never be able to measure the level of our success in every aspect of life. Know this therefore, when people judge you, you must know that you are on the right track. People don't judge what doesn't threaten them. The reason why the other students judge and criticise you is that in you they see a

The Seed became a Forest

potential that they don't see in themselves and for that reason you scare the hell out of them. Now in order for them to feel in charge, they have to suppress your potential before it becomes greater than they can handle. As from today, you must learn to rejoice when people criticise you, it means they can feel your presence and your greatness scares the hell out of them".

The Duke of Happiness

We are all connected

The Seed became a Forest

STIX had just decided to finally go for that job interview and had accepted his boss' offer. As a result of that particular decision, he now has money to send to his mother, who will buy food for STIX's brother and sister. *STIX's* brother will now be happy at school because he had breakfast in the morning. As a result of STIX's brother's happiness, his friends found joy too and they ended up deciding to stay the evening at school studying and practicing mathematics. Their teacher finds it so encouraging that students think of such an important thing and decided to stay with them and help them as much as he can; as a result, they were the highest in mathematics that year. Thank God STIX finally decided to go for that job interview.

On the other side of the story, STIX's wife has afforded to eat healthy at all times and that has kept her into a good shape, which resulted to their relationship being stronger and stronger, as a result, STIX's friend was inspired by how much STIX and his wife love one another, and he also decided to build a similar loving relationship with his wife, instead of spending their

The Duke of Happiness

spare time fighting over things that they didn't even remember in a day's time. So, thanks God STIX decided to go for that job interview, his friend's family happiness has now been restored.

On the other side of the story, STIX was given a full-time company vehicle that he could use to go anywhere he desires. STIX's wife was about to have a baby and thank God STIX had that company vehicle to be able to fetch his wife and their baby from the hospital. On the way home, they decided to pop into the mall to make some shopping. Right before they get into the mall, they come across a poor young man – STONES – who asked for bread. Now, because STIX had decided to go for that job interview, he now has money to give. So, he gave fifty rands to STONES. STONES went home with bread, drink, chicken and snacks that night. As a result of that, STONES's bigger brother – who was a thief for living – didn't have to go out to steal with his buddies that night because STONES had the night covered. In the morning, STONES's brother heard the news that his buddies were shot the previous night, trying to rob a cash transit. All of them were dead. So, thank God STIX decided to go for that job interview, STONES' brother's life is spared.

The Seed became a Forest

On the other side of the story, while STIX was giving that fifty rands to STONES, some beautiful young lady was watching from a distance with amazement. She – ANGELA – was so inspired by STIX's single act of kindness and immediately decided that she will also give something to someone that very night. ANGELA didn't have many friends, even though she had a good and loving heart. She decided to go to the hospital with a lot of fruit in his bag and just give to as many people as possible, especially to those who are not being visited by their relatives. While ANGELA was doing that, one handsome young doctor – BRICKS – was watching with a smile. BRICKS immediately developed an interest in ANGELA. He asked her out and, a few years later, they got married and started a beautiful family. So, thank God STIX finally decided to go for that job interview, ANGELA had finally found the love of her life.

On the other side of the story, BRICKS and ANGELA's son later became a fire fighter and on his third week in the job, he saved 72 people who were trapped into a burning building. So, thank God STIX finally decided to go for that job interview, lives of 72 people were saved from death.

On the other side of the story, one of the 72 people who were saved from burning down with the building was a young man who later got married and his son became the president who gave independence to his country. So, thank God STIX finally went for that job interview, millions of his compatriots are now free people.

The choices that each of us make, affects each and every one of us, either directly or indirectly. We are all connected. We are all different parts of the same thing. What you do will affect me and what I do will affect you. Look at this evidence, I wrote this book and you are reading it. If it inspires you, it will have affected you and your inspiration will affect others.

The Seed became a Forest

The Duke of Happiness

The seed became a forest

The Seed became a Forest

A seed had an idea, its idea was to become a forest. The plans were within the seed, all the patterns and plans of a mighty forest were compressed within that little tiny seed. It knew it won't manifest into a forest overnight and it didn't know HOW it would manifest into that forest. One thing that the seed knew was that it will become a huge forest. That's all it thought, breathed, talked, walked, slept and ate. When the conditions were met, the seed was stuck in the ground, it thought that was the end.

The seed prayed for God to release it because it had a dream of becoming a forest but the more it tried to escape, the more it went deeper and deeper into the ground. Then a big storm came, the seed didn't understand why God was punishing it so much, all it wanted was to become a forest, but God kept it stuck on the ground and exposed it to one hell of a rain. The storm hit the seed so hard that it collapsed.

A couple of days after the storm, the seed woke up to consciousness and realised that it had grown roots. It is

The Duke of Happiness

that day that the seed realised that it needed to be stuck in the ground so in order for its dream to become a reality. It realised also that the storm was not a curse but a blessing in disguise. The seed needed enough water for its roots to grow. The seed then became a tree and that tree bared seeds that later become more trees. Within two decades, the seed had became a forest. All it needed was the conditions to be met. It had no idea what the plan was, it only knew what it wanted.

Within you there is a seed, a plan, an idea, a pattern, a dream, a vision. That dream will come true, it is bound to come true but conditions have to be met. When conditions are met, you will become the person that you had always wanted to be. You will have the things that you had always wanted to have. You will do what you had always wanted to do.

The Seed became a Forest

The delivery boy that became a manager

The Seed became a Forest

This is how my seed became a mighty forest. I remember when I used to work as a delivery boy at builders warehouse. I was earning such a small amount of money and I had to support my family from it, as little as it was. During the entire period of time I worked there, I knew at every minute from the bottom of my heart that *"this is not where I belong"*. I used to look at the other delivery boys and think to myself *"I can't believe I'm one of them"*. Yes, I know that sounds judgemental but, I was one of them, so there is no way I were able to judge them.

Anyway, I knew that I had a higher and greater purpose in life. I knew in my heart that I was destined for greater things. I didn't know what I was destined for. For a moment I awaited a "sign". And time went by without any appearance of any sort of sign. This one lousy sunshiny day, something happened. We were delivering a load of 50Kg cement bags and there were only four of us. Our destination was a construction site on the other side of the road from Coca cola warehouse. As I were busy off loading, I couldn't help noticing this gentleman who had just parked his white Isuzu double cab

The Duke of Happiness

4x4 280KB in front of a network site in the premises of Coca cola. I stopped and looked carefully as this dude opened the door, got off and slammed the door, wearing a navy overall work suit, black safety boots, and spectacles on his eyes and carrying a laptop. I analyzed every single detail with this bro. About 4 meters away from the car, he held the car alarm remote over his shoulder and pressed it *(locked the doors).* And then went to open the network site which I later noticed it had an MTN sign on the gate.

At that moment, I knew I *definitely* had a purpose in life and my purpose was to become *"that man"*. From that day on, I held a picture of that man in my mind, nothing else. Every morning when I woke up and every night before I go to sleep, I would imagine myself as *"that man"*. For a good couple of months, nothing dramatic happened. At the beginning of the year 2008, my father passed away (*more about this in the TINSTAHL*). My mother advised me to visit the telecommunications company that my father used to work for and tell them who I am, about my father's passing away and also ask them if they don't have a job for me. I had their number and I phoned them. But – unfortunately – they didn't

The Seed became a Forest

have any work for me, but were to call me as soon as something comes up. After a couple of weeks, my mother told me to phone them again and ask how things stood. I phoned them and they told me to come on Monday for an interview. I took a day off at builder's warehouse and went to that Telecommunications Company. Mind you, I had never been there before but I didn't struggle a bit finding the place. It was like I was led there.

I got there and asked for the boss. I told him who I was and what I visited him for. To respect his identity, I will call him Patrick. So, Patrick told me he would make me an Installer. Later in our conversation, he discovered that I were very good with computers and immediately decided to make me a Technician. Only to find out, they had an open position for a qualified Technician. They were looking for someone with some degree in Telecommunications, with three to five years experience in the field and with the driver's license. I had NEITHER of the above. Patrick summoned the manager – (To respect the Manager's identity, I will call him Shakes) – and told him who I was and that he was to make me a Telecommunications Technician. Shakes was pleased

The Duke of Happiness

and he told me also that, *"it isn't a rocket science"* if I knew my computer, then I were to be just fine. Shakes, the manager, then left the office. Just after Shakes had left, Patrick said to me *"But then you do know that you're obviously going start at the bottom, right?"*. Then I said *"Of course Sir"*. Patrick then told me to come start on the following Monday. Monday came and when I got to the work place, Patrick was not in the office, he was in Johannesburg for business and would be back in two weeks time.

Now, when Shakes found me down stairs, he told me that I wasn't supposed to be there, I was supposed to go upstairs, Patrick said he wanted me to be a Technician (of course Shakes didn't hear the part where I start at the bottom and work my way up). I told myself that I only had two weeks to prove my ability to become a Technician, before the boss comes back. In a period of two weeks, I performed very well and when the boss came back, he received a very good feedback about my performance. And, by default, he thought I was perfect where I was (*to hell with starting at the bottom...lol*).

The Seed became a Forest

I instantly became a Technician and I had a driver to drive me around – I had no driver's license. And my performance became better and better. After a year, I went for my driver's license and I passed it, thank you God!

So, I became good at what I do. I was the master of the Ericsson Node B software. Even MTN Technicians would phone me for assistance if they were having trouble with the software on site. Anyway, I loved what I was doing and I did it with passion. So, now that I had a driver's license, they would send me to sites by myself and here is where miracle started to happen, the vehicle I was issued was a white Isuzu double cab 4x4. The company's overalls were navy and I was issued safety boots. These things didn't blow my mind as yet, my mind hadn't noticed them. I went to sites, I installed the Ericsson 3G, I did upgrades from site to site all over the Western Province and I still hadn't noticed anything.

Until this one sunshiny day; when I was asked to go insert a RAX board in a 3G system at Coca Cola beverages. I didn't know where the site was, so I took the GPS and punched in the co-ordinates.

The Duke of Happiness

The GPS took me to Coca Cola beverages and just after parking the van, I remembered that I was here before. I looked across the road and I noticed that there was a new building. Wait a second, this is the building I was delivering cement at, when I saw that guy wearing a navy overall with safety boots, carrying a laptop and driving a white Isuzu double cab 4x4. The very same guy I made up my mind that I wanted to be. Then I looked at myself, starting from my feet, I was wearing a black pair of safety boots, a navy overall, I was carrying a laptop and I was driving a white Isuzu double cab 4x4.

Am I dreaming?

I started wondering. Then I couldn't help my tears from falling. Truly and truly, God does answer our prayers, we just need to know what we want and be patient enough to wait for it. I was that guy, without even realizing it. Later I resigned from that company and got a job at a similar company as a junior project manager. I worked there for two years. The guy I dreamt of becoming was now reporting to me. Then at the beginning of my third year in this company, I got an offer from an international telecommunications company to be a

The Seed became a Forest

Provincial Project Manager. I was now issuing jobs to the smaller companies. One of the companies that reported to me was the very company that gave me my very first telecommunications job.

Remember, I had no qualifications, no experience and no driver's license. The only thing I had was a dream. When conditions are met, a seed can truly become a forest.

The Duke of Happiness

Words from The Duke:

Thank you for reading this book. I hope and trust that it had touched your heart, inspired your soul and changed your life.

Please give us a feedback:
Facebook: The Duke Publishers
*   The Duke of Happiness*
*   #I_AM_THE_LIGHT*

Twitter: @MeTheDuke

www.ingramcontent.com/pod-product-compliance
Lightning Source LLC
Chambersburg PA
CBHW070516090426
42735CB00012B/2802